Living and Nonliving in the

Grasslands

Rebecca Rissman

Heinemann
LIBRARY
Chicago, Illinois

To contact Capstone Global Library please phone
800-747-4992, or visit our website
www.capstonepub.com

Edited by Daniel Nunn, Rebecca Rissman, and
Catherine Veitch
Designed by Cynthia Della-Rovere
Picture research by Tracy Cummins
Production by Sophia Argyris
Originated by Capstone Global Library Ltd
Printed and bound in China by Leo Paper Products Ltd

ISBN 978-1-4109-5384-1 (hc)
ISBN 978-1-4109-5391-9 (pb)
17 16 15 14 13
10 9 8 7 6 5 4 3 2 1

Library of Congress Cataloging-in-Publication Data

Rissman, Rebecca.
  Living and nonliving in the grasslands / Rebecca Rissman.
    pages cm.—(Is it living or nonliving?)
  Includes bibliographical references and index.
  ISBN 978-1-4109-5384-1 (hb)—ISBN 978-1-4109-
5391-9 (pb) 1. Grasslands—Juvenile literature. 2. Life
(Biology)—Juvenile literature. I. Title.

  QH87.7.R57 2013
  577.4—dc23   2012046872

Acknowledgments

We would like to thank the following for permission to
reproduce photographs: istockphoto pp. 9 (© Richard
Gillard), 22 (© Justin Matley); Shutterstock pp. 1, 19
(© Maksym Protsenko), 4, 23b (© Vadim Petrakov), 5
(© l i g h t p o e t), 6, 23d (© Galyna Andrushko), 7
(© Amelandfoto), 8, 23c (© Pavelk), 10 (© Jason
Prince), 11 (© Dave Pusey), 12 (© Anna Diederich), 14
(© Simon_g), 15 (© Tony Campbell), 16 (© Sinelyov),
18 (© Mazzzur), 20, 23a (© Slawek Kuter), 21 (© Alta
Oosthuizen); Superstock pp. 13 (© Peter Blahut/All Canada
Photos), 17 (Cusp).

Front cover photograph of an African elephant reproduced
with permission of Superstock (© Corbis).

We would like to thank Michael Bright and Nancy Harris for
their invaluable help in the preparation of this book.

Every effort has been made to contact copyright holders
of material reproduced in this book. Any omissions will be
rectified in subsequent printings if notice is given to the
publisher.

All the Internet addresses (URLs) given in this book were
valid at the time of going to press. However, due to the
dynamic nature of the Internet, some addresses may
have changed, or sites may have changed or ceased to
exist since publication. While the author and publisher
regret any inconvenience this may cause readers, no
responsibility for any such changes can be accepted by
either the author or the publisher.

Some words are in bold, **like this**.
You can find them in the glossary on page 23.

0 1021 0281719 8

Contents

What Is a Grassland?

A grassland is a large area of land covered in grasses. Grasslands have few trees.

Different types of plants and animals live in grasslands.

There are **nonliving** things in grasslands too.

What Are Living Things?

Living things are alive. Living things need air and **sunlight**. Living things move on their own.

Living things grow and change.

Living things need food and water.

What Are Nonliving Things?

Nonliving things are not alive. Nonliving things do not need air and **sunlight**.

Nonliving things do not need food or water.

nonliving

Nonliving things do not grow and change on their own.

Nonliving things do not move on their own.

Is a Lion Living or Nonliving?

A lion needs food and water.

A lion moves on its own.

A lion grows and changes.

A lion needs air and **sunlight**.

A lion is **living**.

Is a Rock Living or Nonliving?

A rock does not move on its own.

A rock does not grow and change on its own.

A rock does not need food or water.

A rock does not need air or **sunlight**.

A rock is **nonliving**.

Is a Bird Living or Nonliving?

A bird grows and changes.

A bird moves on its own.

A bird needs food and water.

A bird needs air and **sunlight**.

A bird is **living**.

Is Soil Living or Nonliving?

Soil does not move on its own.

Soil does not need food or water.

Soil does not grow and change on its own.

Soil does not need air and **sunlight**.

Soil is **nonliving**.

Is Grass Living or Nonliving?

Grass grows and changes.

Grass needs water.

Grass moves on its own toward the sun.

Grass needs air and **sunlight**.

Grass is **living**.

Is a Grasshopper Living or Nonliving?

A **grasshopper** moves on its own.

A grasshopper needs food and water.

A grasshopper grows and changes.

A grasshopper needs air and **sunlight**.

A grasshopper is **living**.

What Do You Think?

Is this stream **living** or **nonliving**?

Glossary

grasshopper type of insect that can jump very high

living alive. Living things need food and water. They breathe and move on their own. They grow and change.

nonliving not alive. Nonliving things do not need food and water. They do not move on their own. They do not grow and change on their own.

sunlight light from the sun

Find Out More

Websites

Facthound offers a safe, fun way to find Internet sites related to this book. All of the sites on Facthound have been researched by our staff.

Here's all you do:
Visit www.facthound.com
Type in this code: 9781410953841

Books

Lindeen, Carol K. *Living and Nonliving*. Mankato, Minn.: Capstone, 2008.

Silverman, Buffy. *Grasslands (Habitat Survival)*. Chicago: Raintree, 2013.

Underwood, Deborah. *Hiding in Grasslands*. Chicago: Heinemann, 2011.

Index